We Love Because ...

We Love Because
Published by Ray Hawkins
Typesetting by Book Whispers
Copyright Ray Hawkins 2014.

P.O. Box 379 Beauty Point Tasmania
Email   ray.haw3819@bigpond.com
http://rayhawkinsauthor.blogspot.com.au

National Library of Australia Cataloguing-in-Publication entry

Author: Hawkins, Ray, author.
Title: We love because ... : celebrating 50 years / Ray Hawkins.
ISBN: 9781921632990 (paperback)
Subjects: Marriage--Poetry.
             Wedding anniversaries--Poetry.
Dewey Number: A821.4

All rights reserved. No part of this publication may be reproduced, stored in, or introduced into a retrieval system, or transmitted, in any form, or by any means (electronic, mechanical, photocopying, recording or otherwise) without the prior written permission of the publisher.

We Love Because ...

A husband's reflection of falling in love and staying in love with his wife

Contents

We Love Because …	i
We Love Because …	iii
Love Defined	1
The Dream of the Heart	3
I Liked You	5
I Didn't Fall in Love	7
The Prisoner	9
Hands Entwined	11
This Is a Promise I Can Make You	12
We Call It Beautiful	14
I'd Rather …	16
Into Your Hands	18
Wedding Covenant	20
Every Day Love	22
I Hear Your Voice of Love	24
I Cannot Pretend to Love	26
The Language of Christian Love	28
My Dream of Love	30
Dancing with Fire	31
Love Songs Have Eternity in Them	33
Kiss it Better	35
Time Changes Love	37
Sweet Memories	39
No Words Said	40
Together	41
The Night of the Golden Moon	43
I Thought I Loved You	44
The Heart Whispers	46
Forget You? Possibly	48
Come to My Arms	50

Each and Every Day	51
I Don't See …	53
I Never Get Tired of …	54
I'm Too Weak	56
The Wife's Returning	58
Mary, my Mary, Come With Me	60
O Laama O Laama	62
Rainbow in the Mist	64
Thank You, Thank You	66
You Were There	68
The Gambler	70
You, Me and the Letter 'V'	72
The Photograph	73
I Forgot to Remember	75
Background Music	77
Funny Isn't It	78
Green Eyed Fire	79
You're Always In My Heart	80
Looking Back on Love	82
Love Thoughts	83
One Day at a Time	84
The Seat in the Park	85
It Hasn't Been Easy	87
We Love Because …	89
How Can it Be	90

Love Defined

The Lord Jesus commands me to love whether you are friend or enemy, spouse or child. Love is such a funny all embracing word that can mean anything or nothing. It depends upon the intent of the person and the underpinning convictions of the heart.

Love is actually the reflection of a personal experience of God's love.

This flows from our knowledge of and commitment to Christ Jesus as Lord and Saviour. From that encounter love, as defined by the Lord, seeks to express itself. Love reaches out to others with genuineness and without hidden agendas.

Therefore, what do I mean when I say "I love you?"

Love is to touch you at the level of our relationship in a manner pleasing to our Lord.

Love seeks to hear your heart and not simply respond to the words of your mouth.

Love will allow you space to be yourself and yet help you to be what you want to be.

Love sits with you in your tears, cries with you and offers both the heart and the hand.

Love stands with you in your circumstances.

Love walks with you into life's uncertainties.

Love dances with you in your celebrations and joys.

Love endeavours to provide for your well–being.

Love will confront error without being judgemental.

Love reaches out with forgiveness even from a wounded heart.

Love gives even when it is misunderstood, scorned or exploited.

Love is more than a word.

It is a world coloured by the discovery of the Love of God expressed at Calvary. Love is saturated by His power to redeem, restore and renew. Such indwelling love cannot be imprisoned. It must weave its grace and power in and through the personality, abilities and opportunities of the lover to the one loved.

We love because He (God) first loved us. 1 John 4:19.

The Dream of the Heart

Through adolescent imagination,
Across emotional isolation,
Despite swirling consternation,
A dream was born.
Love's longing,
Heart's yearning
To love,
Be loved,
Uniquely,
Fervently,
Eternally!

Through darkest nights,
Across spreading years,
Despite deepest fears,
The dream lingered.
Love's longing,
Heart's yearning
To love,
Be loved,
Undeniably,
Unrelentingly,
Unashamedly!

To Heaven I cried.
To Heaven I bowed.
To Heaven I vowed,
My life
My all
To see,
To feel
My dreams come true.

Through Heaven's providence
Across Earth's continents
Despite Human impudence,
My dream came true.
Love's longing
Heart's yearning
To love,
Be loved,
    Realised
    Personalised
      Satisfied ...
        In you!

I Liked You

I liked you
The moment I met you
So gracious,
Vivacious,
I was drawn to you.
You attracted
My attention,
Though I had no intention
Of being
Captured
By anyone at all.

It's unfair
Oh so unfair
To these eyes of mine
You're so attractive
And appealing
To these eyes of mine.

I missed you
The moment you left me
Loneliness,
Emptiness,
Those strange sensations
Arrested me,
Confused me,
Their vacuum overwhelmed me.
I cried.
I waited
Longing for your return.

It's unfair
Oh so unfair
To these arms of mine.
You're embraceable
So delectable
In these arms of mine.

I loved you
Long before I kissed you
My desire
Set on fire
By your enticing
Flashing eyes.
Enraptured
My life was yours evermore.
Saturated,
Infatuated
You're my heart's obsession.

It's unfair,
Oh so unfair,
To this heart of mine
You're spell-binding
Mystifying
To this heart of mine!

I Didn't Fall in Love

I didn't fall in love
As though it was
An accident.
I didn't fall for you
To be forever prostrate.
I didn't fall
I wasn't pushed
No
I didn't fall
In love with you!

I walked into love
It was a path
Of discovery
Seeing you
Appreciating you.
Encouraged by friends
Sensing God's pleasure
I began to watch you
And it seems
You watched me.
Tentatively
Our hands reached out
Touched
Our walk began
Together
Without stopping.

I didn't fall in love
I walked into love
As I knew you

I became captive
Yet strangely free
To be really me
When with you!
I reached out
And found
Your hand
Reaching for mine
To walk into love
Together
Forever!

The Prisoner

Arrested!
No resistance.
Confession unforced.
The charge –
Heart
Stolen
Affections
Seized!

No parole
Granted
No pardon
Sought –
Chains invisible
Hold fast.
Bars unseeable
Embrace
A life sentence,
Without remissions,
Without escape,
Confine this prisoner.
No guards
Patrol
No walls
Surround –
Intangible
Security
Indefinable
Protection.
The heart's assurance
Without pretension

Without deception
Envelope this prisoner.

Love makes
Lovers prisoners.
Freedom
Unwanted
Vows
Sanctified
Dreams
Satisfied!

Hands Entwined

A walk in the park
Not quite dark
Two friends stride
Side by side.
He, bashful
She, beautiful
And demure.

Hands collide
Intent implied.
Cheeks blush
Pulses rush.
Fingers stretch,
Lightly touch
Linger
Link.

A walk through years,
Not without tears,
Two lovers striding
Hands still holding
He, resourceful
She, thoughtful
With allure.
Hands entwined,
Faces that shine
A love divine
Sweeter than wine
Intoxicating
Celebrating
Hearts
Combined.

This Is a Promise I Can Make You

The impossible is so easily promised,
Love songs do it all the time.
Each fear calmed, every tear wiped,
No hurts felt, anger never present.
Such love is beyond who I am,
However,
This I can promise you ...
    To honour you with integrity
    To safeguard your dignity
    To love you with fidelity

The impossible I cannot offer
As much as I would so will it.
Weariness often deafens me,
Self pity can wound intimacy,
Pride breeds independency
However,
This I can promise you ...
    To seek your forgiveness
    To enhance your loveliness
    To appreciate your tenderness.

The impossible I cannot undertake,
To say anything else is a mistake.
Marital harmony suffers discords,
There'll be things we can't afford.
Expectation will clash, crash.
However,

This I can promise you ...
    To walk with you in fellowship
    To kneel with you in our worship
    To serve with you in discipleship.

The impossible I cannot fulfil.
Such love songs I'll never sing.
There will be periods of pain,
  Mingled with joyous strains
As life's uncertainties intrude.
    However,
This I can promise you ...
    To consider you my treasure
    To delight in your pleasure
    To love you beyond measure

We Call It Beautiful

We call it beautiful, so ...

It's woven within a sunrise,
Spreads itself through a valley,
Dances through a waterfall
And shines on a moonlit night!
We call it beautiful.
But ...
Beauty is experienced
More than seen
A matter of the heart
More than the eyes!
So, when I say
You're beautiful
It is my heart
Moving my lips
Because of what
I see!

It's seen in the joy of a blue wren
Hopping with his mate,
The fragrance of a rose in bloom
Permeates the air with perfume!
We call it beautiful.
But ...
Beauty is enjoyable
More than debated
A matter of the spirit
More than reason!
So, when I say
You're beautiful

It is my spirit
Expressing joy
Because of what
I see!

It's captured by an artist's brush
Portraits enriched by time,
Spying a spider's winter web
Captivates the imagination!
We call it beautiful.
But ...
Beauty is mystery
More than words
A matter of rapport
More than logic!
So, when I say
You're beautiful
It is my being
Knowing true love
Because of what
I see!

I'd Rather...

I'd rather hold your hand
In the dark,
Than,
Walk in the sunshine
Without you.

I'd rather grow old with you
In marriage
Than,
Taste eternal youthfulness
Without you.

I'd rather be materially poor
With your love
Than,
Financially rich but
Without you.

Why?
Because!
I cannot live
Without my heart.
You are my heart!

I'd rather share your sorrows
Every day
Than,
Living carelessly
Never helping you.

I'd rather be a nobody
In this world

Than,
Famous and feted
Never knowing you.

I'd rather die
As your husband
Than,
Live forever
Never loving you.

Why?
Because,
I cannot deny
You're God's gift,
His treasure to me!

Into Your Hands

December 19th 1964
Your hands took mine
Quietly,
Tenderly,
Firmly.
That day began,
For us, God's plan,
A walk together,
Lover's before God,
Friends within God,
Minister's serving God,
Hand in hand.

December 19th 1964
Your hands took mine
Covenanting,
Caressing,
Confirming
Matrimony's bond.
Something sublime,
God's design
Across all time.
Its magnitude
We'll explore
Hand in hand.

December 19th 2004
Your hands still hold mine
Lovingly,
Joyfully,
Creatively.

Years, our privilege,
To know the wonder,
God's pleasure
Safeguarding,
Undergirding,
Upholding,
Hand in hand.

December 19th onwards
Your hands hold mine
Unashamedly,
Confidently,
Courageously.
A never ending grip
Love's companionship
God's calling.
Beyond life,
Through death,
With Jesus
Hand in hand.

Wedding Covenant

My heart was pulsating
As I took your hand
A tear filled my eye,
A sigh fled my lips
When I placed
The ring
On your finger.

With this ring,
I thee wed
Was my covenant
To you.

With this ring
I thee wed
Was your covenant
To me.

Heaven's purpose,
Earth's passion
Blended,
Made splendid
In the kiss
That sealed
Our wedding covenant.

Lord,
On this special day
Our desire is,
To know,
To taste,
To live

Earth's undying desire,
Heaven's undiminished fire,
Love's unfading pleasure,
Love's unfailing treasure,
Two lives becoming one!

Lord,
On this special day,
Hear our plea,
To know
The heights,
The depths,
The wonder,
Two lives becoming one
Earth's undying desire,
Heaven's undiminished fire,
Love's unfading pleasure,
Love's unfailing treasure,
Two lives becoming one!

Every Day Love

Whether in garden shoes,
Soiled blouse,
Jeans,
Or
Tuxedo and tails
Bowtie
Top hat ...
Love remains unchanged
Behind each fashion
That covered
The one loved.

Whether at kitchen table
With sandwiches
Ice cream,
Or
High class dining
A la carte
Cuisine ...
Love remains satisfied
In the company
That nurtured
The one loved.

Whether in honeymoon mode
Togetherness
Insatiable
Or
Under family pressures
Togetherness
Unrealised ...

Love remains vibrant
Confirming,
Enabling
The one loved.

I Hear Your Voice of Love

I hear the voice of your love
Falling on my heart and mind,
Sometimes soft as a snow flake
Other times a fire's warm glow.

I feel the voice of your love
Cascading over my soul,
Sometimes refreshing as tea
Or stimulating as coffee!

Your love speaks to me
Through your commitment
   To me
     Our children
     And ministry
         A holy statement
         Of Heaven's intent!

Your love speaks to me
Through your faithfulness
   To me
     Our children
     And ministry
         A holy expression
         With Heaven's intent!

Your love speaks to me
Through your self denial
   To me
     Our children
     And ministry
         A holy surrender
         To Heaven's intent!

Your love speaks to me
Through your strong passions
To me
Our children
And ministry
A holy testimony
From Heaven's intent!

I Cannot Pretend to Love

Some songs tell us to pretend,
To make believe
We're in love.
Some songs want us to live lies
And they wonder
Why love dies.

Love is too precious for that,
The heart is too fragile for lies,
Love is more gracious than that.
The mind is so tender it hurts
When it feels the words untrue,
Love is too special for that.

When I look into your eyes
And whisper in your ears
That I love you, love you,
I'm not pretending.
There's no make believe
In what I say,
No deceiving with words
When I write to say,
I love you, love you.

I could never pretend to love.
I could never make believe
The love I have for you.
This is my confession,
You are my obsession,
I am your possession
And I'm not pretending.

When you take my hand
Look into my eyes
And feel my lips
You'll understand
I'm not pretending
Of love unending
I have for you.

The Language of Christian Love

Christian love has a language.
Heaven's vocabulary
Earth's signage
Revealing grace
That's Christ's love!
That's Agape!*
Love unfading
Love unfailing
Love unfolding

Christian love has a language.
Culturally understood,
Embracing all
Offering grace
That's Christ's love!
That's Agape!
Love renewing.
Love restoring.
Love refreshing

Christian love has a language.
Explained by Jesus
At Calvary
Unleashing grace
That's Christ's love!
That's Agape!

Love exciting
Love enriching
Love enticing

*Agape is an ancient Greek word which the first generation of Christians considered most appropriate and applied it to God. (John 3:16) It expresses His desire to show it within the lives of all who claim Jesus as their Lord and Saviour. (1 Corinthians 13)

My Dream of Love

There are those who say
Love is but a fantasy
Beautiful and unreal
If this be so
Let me seek its mythology
For I'm in love with you!

There are those who say
Love is a memory
A strange wonderland
If this be so
Let me search its mystery
For I'm in love with you!

There are those who say
Love is just a sonnet
Words made to rhyme
If this be so
Let me make it sublime
For I'm in love with you!

You,
You are my dream of love,
Its sweet mystery!
You,
You are my sonnet of love,
Its sweet fantasy!
You,
You are my song of love,
Its sweet melody,
For,
I'm in love with you!

Dancing with Fire

I look into you eyes
And I see
The music of romance
Calling me
To give myself to you
In the rhythm of the dance

When you hold me
In your arms
The rhythm of romance
Waltzes me
To surrender to you
In the music of the dance.

I look into your eyes
And I see
The flames of romance
Drawing me
To give myself to you
In the tempo of the dance.

When you take me
In your arms
The delight of romance
Captures me
To move as one with you
In the story of the dance.

I look into you eyes
And I see
The wonder of romance
Leading me

To give myself to you
In the glory of the dance.

I want to dance
To the music
In our hearts
I want to move
To the rhythm
Of our romance
Today
To night
For ever!

Love Songs Have Eternity in Them

Do love songs ever die?
Suffer decay
Death's dust!
Are love songs phantoms
Of imagination,
Wild emotions
Softly told lies
To beguile!
Is there Forever Love
Out there,
Somewhere!

Can love songs never die?
Unchanged
Unchained?
Are love's songs Eternal
Reality,
Faithful
Truthful
Beautiful?
Is there Forever Love
From above
To within!

Where love songs never die
Beyond earth,
Above sky
Is true love's paradise
Undefiled,

Glorified,
Realised,
Satisfied.
Here is Forever Love,
Christ
Jesus.

Real love songs never die
When life ends
Worlds cease
True Love's song is of God
The Creator,
Perfector,
Provider,
Protector
He is Forever Love
To us
In grace.

This is separate. Originally I had it attached but Mary thought it was best to stand alone.

Love songs are words woven
With eternity in them.
For love is of God
He is eternal.
We by faith
Belong to Him
So the songs we sing
Will never cease.
There in glory
We will rehearse
Love songs for Him,
Together,
Forever.

Kiss it Better

Kiss it better
This hurting heart of mine.
Kiss it better
Is my plea.
Only you can heal
This aching
Breaking
Heart of mine.

When I was young,
So very young,
Mother would say to me,
"Come here my dear,
Let me kiss it better."

Now I'm older,
So much older
Lover, please say to me,
"Come here my love,
Let me kiss it better."

Kiss it better
This pain deep within
Kiss it better
Is my cry
Only you can ease
This sadness,
Sickness
Deep within.

Kiss it better
This heart of mine

Kiss it better
With lips divine.
Heal the emptiness.
Cure the loneliness
With your nectar
Kiss me better
Oh!
Kiss me better
And this I'll promise.
I'll do
The same
To you!

Time Changes Love

Time,
Such a change agent
Leaves nothing untouched
Not even love.
Time
Gives us wrinkles
Increases girths
Slows activity
Time
Never stands still
Never retreats
Never apologises.

Time
Should make love deepen
Affection stronger
Passion sweeter.
Time
Gives us a chance
To mend faults
Forgive failures.
Time,
Blesses mercy
Blesses kindness
Blesses justice

Time
Offers new seasons
To be enjoyed
And explored
Time

Can enrich love
With memories
Shared histories
Time
Deepens trust
Deepens grace
Deepens love

O that I may
Make the most
Of my time
To love
You!

Sweet Memories

Sitting here
You saw me,
Laughing,
Crying,
Dreaming,
Sighing
As I held
Precious memories.

Love letters you'd sent.
Photographs, some bent,
Corny birthday cards
Items for the yard
O so many things
With me to arouse
Memories.

Watching me
Your smile
Beguiling
Presence
Bewitching,
Thrilled me
As I held
Precious history.

Special souvenirs
From places far, near
Journeys we'd taken,
Compassions awakened
O so many things
That made us create
Memories.

No Words Said

No words were said,
Yet he knew.
She looked.
The unsaid
Was said.

Invisible,
Powerful,
Wordless
Communication
Connected.
Sparkling eyes,
Tilted eyebrow,
Wrinkled nose,
Furrowed brow,
Shaped lips
Sent messages,
Strong,
Silent,
Suggestive.

No words replied
Yet she knew.
He looked.
The unsaid
Replied.

Together

Together,
We've walked
Through the years
And
Struggled
Through our tears
Together.

We've faced
The winds
Of adversity
And rested
In the calm
Of prosperity
Together.

Through it all
You stood by me,
Prayed for me,
Loved me
Through it all!

Together,
We've tasted
The wine of Heaven
And
We've sipped
The gall of the world
Together.

We've dreamed
The dreams

Of achievement
And waited
In the joy
Of contentment
Together.

Through it all
You walked with me
Protected me
Lifted me
Through it all

Together,
We've climbed
Life's difficulties
And
We've mastered
Doubt's uncertainties
Together.

We've served
The Lord
In His calling
And known
The wonder
Of His blessing
Together.

Through it all
We've stood together
Through it all
We've loved each other
Through it all
Together!

The Night of the Golden Moon

It was September
In Australia
When we walked together
Beneath the golden moon.
The stars winked their pleasure
At each other
As two lovers
Walked hand in hand
Beneath the glowing moon

I'll long remember
That September
When we walked together
Beneath the golden moon.
My mind contains the fire
Fuels desire
For two lovers
Still hand in hand
Beneath the glowing moon.

It's always September
In Australia
When we walk together
Beneath the golden moon
Memories bloom
For two lovers
Now aging
Still hand in hand
Beneath the glowing moon.

I Thought I Loved You

Those many years ago,
When we met,
Walked together
Across time
I thought I loved you.
I was wrong!
Well,
Maybe not wrong, wrong
But I'd have to say,
In the light of day
How I feel today
Makes
Yesteryear's love
A mere shadow
Of love's reality.

In twenty years time,
Should God allow,
Comparing then, now
Perhaps,
I'll scratch my head,
You'll hear it said,
"I was wrong",
Well,
Maybe not wrong, wrong
Those many years ago
But compared to now,
Did I really know
What I was on about
When I said,
"I love you?"

I thought I loved you
Those years ago
I was wrong,
Well,
Maybe not wrong, wrong
It was love's infancy
Love's innocence
Now,
Life tested
Love has maturity
So ...
I can honestly say
This very day,
I wasn't wrong, wrong
When I said
"I love you"

The Heart Whispers

The story of our love
Can never be told
Without God's grace.
He sealed our destiny
Gave us a unity
Wrapt in His love.
For when I looked at you
My heart whispered
To my mind,
Love,
Love has just begun.

The story of our love
Will never be told
Without God grace.
He calmed our calamities
Restored our sanity
Wrapt in His love.
And when I looked at you
My heart whispered
To my mind,
Love,
Love gave our life fun.

The story of our love
Should never be told
Outside God's grace.
Across life's many journeys
His presence we knew
Wrapt in His love.
And when I look at you

My heart whispered
To my mind
Love,
Love still keeps us young.

The story of our love
Can never be told
Outside God's grace
He bonded us together
Through all the years
Wrapt in His love.
And when I look at you
My heart still whispers
To my mind
Love,
Love has just begun!

Forget You? Possibly

Forget you, my beloved?
Possibly
Unintentionally,
But,
Possibly.
Years overtake
Memory wanders
Yesteryears forgotten
So,
Tearfully,
Forgetting you could be a possibility!

Forget you, my beloved?
Only outwardly,
Never inwardly.
You
Fashioned me,
Ennobled me
Loved me completely
Helped me greatly
And,
Therefore,
Forgetting you is an impossibility!

Forget you my beloved?
While our heart pulses
And our mind functions
Let's,
Imprint them
With memories,
Pleasant melodies,

Tender mercies,
Which
Ensures
Forgetting each other's an impossibility!

Forget you my beloved?
Temporarily,
Not eternally.
God's
Promises
Safeguards our Love
Through mental robbery,
To be reclaimed
Where
Together,
Forgetting is an impossibility!

Come to My Arms

When life's storms howl
And sorrows growl
Hide in my arms
Away from what alarms

Come,
Come to my arms
Let them uphold you
Faithfully
Come,
Come to my arms
Let them surround you
Tenderly.

Come,
Come to my arms,
Let them enfold you
Strongly
Come,
Come to my arms,
Let them embrace you
Lovingly.

In my arms you will find
Strength renewed,
Peace restored
Amidst all that alarms.

Each and Every Day

I read it every day
Of people who don't care
For one they use to love.
Sadness fills my mind
Reading such despair
For I can truly say
Each and every day,
I love you more and more.

Each and every day
I thank Heaven above
For the wonder of your love
Through the good times.
Through the tough times
Come what may,
You've stood with me,
Hand in hand,
Heart with heart
Each and every day.

I hear it every day
From people so depressed
For a love that has died.
Sadness fills my heart
Hearing so much distress
But it makes me pray
Each and every day
To love you more and more.

Each and every day
I thank the Lord above
For the comfort of your love.

Through the good times,
Through the tough times
Let me say
You've walked with me
Hand in hand,
Heart with heart
Each and every day.

That is why I can say,
Each and every day,
In so many ways,
I love you so much more
Than the day before!

I Don't See ...

I don't see the grey in your hair,
Lines around sparkling eyes
Nor the slowness of your pace
Lilting laughter,
Radiant face,
Hide all that from me.

I don't hear the stutter of voice,
Words sometimes hard to frame
Sport may be beyond us both
But your embrace,
Tender kiss,
Hide all that from me.

I don't notice passing years
Or fret over changing shapes
Sleep may be spasmodic,
Still, the faith shared
Fun enjoyed
Hide all that from me.

I don't doubt some imagine
I'm short-sighted, deaf.
The pictures we've painted
Throughout our years,
Adorning our hearts
Hide all that from me.

I Never Get Tired of...

I never get tired of hearing you say
"I – love – you!"
I never get weary of seeing it's true
Night and day,
So many ways,
You seem to say
"I – love – you!"

In the darkest times
When sorrow is high
Through day and night
Of the toughest fight,
As spirit sighs,
Shoulders sag
Your caressing eyes
Re–assuring words,
Makes me strong again.

When my body's aching,
My mind is spinning
From daily burdens
And family hurdles
You hold me near,
Calming fears
Your tender touch
Encouraging me,
Makes me strong again.

I never get tired of hearing you say
"I – love – you!"
I will never tire of seeing it's true
Night and day,

In many ways,
You seem to say
"I – love – you!"

Yes, I'll say it again and again
I – love - you
In a hundred and one different ways,
Night and day,
Come what may,
I want to say
"I – love – you!"

I'm Too Weak

The life I'm called to live,
The journey I must take,
Is too hard,
Too long
For me.
My strength is unable
My faith is unstable
I fear I will fall
And not rise again
On my own.

I need you to walk with me
And be my company.
I need you to hold my hand
To love and understand.
Some see me as 'oh so strong'
But see not the agony
Of taunting memory
deep within,
deep within.

The way I'm called to walk.
The pathway I must take
Is too high
Too tough
For me.
My mind sees danger
My heart feels terror
It knows I can fail
In the journey
On my own.

I need you to walk with me
And be my company.
I need you to refresh me
To guide and lift me.
Someday at journey's end
I will look at you and say,
"Your love and company
Made me strong,
Made me strong!"

The Wife's Returning

Oh no!
She's due home tonight.
What'll I do?
Where do I start?
I confess,
The place's a mess.
She'll have a fright
To see this sight.
Hugs, kisses, frozen
Due to my dozin'.
Dishes unwashed.
Bed unmade.
Papers scattered ...
I need a maid!

Body, get moving.
Brain, into gear.
Muscles, strain.
The cleaning begins.
Plates, cups, pans
Spick and span
Floor vacuumed
Sofa combed,
Order restored,
Flowers installed,
Odours cleansed ...
But not from me.

Door bells chime
Is it that time?
I struggle there,

Bump a chair,
Almost swear.
My pulse beats.
I open the door ...
The neighbour smiles
I feel riled.
"Your wife rang,
Your phone's unplugged
Here's her message."...

It read,
Darling,
I'm delayed
Just a few days.
Sorry!
Keep your smile,
That's your style
Only a little while
So don't moan and groan
I'll soon be home!

P.S.
I forgot to say
Ere I went away
I'd arranged
Home cleaning
For the morning
To save you the worry!
So terribly sorry
Love.
xxxx.

Aaaaaaahhhhhhhhh!

Mary, my Mary, Come With Me

Mary, my fair Mary
Will you come and talk with me?
I have things to say to you
In words of love soft and true.
Mary, my fair Mary,
Will you come and talk with me?

Mary, my sweet Mary
Will you come and walk with me?
There are things I'll show to you
Along paths with changing views.
Mary, my sweet Mary,
Will you come and walk with me?

Mary, my strong Mary
Will you came and work with me?
I have things from God to do
In ministries and I need you.
Mary, my strong Mary,
Will you come and work with me?

Mary, my brave Mary
You've talked, walked, worked with me
In Christ's grace and integrity
As God's gift to my ministry.
Mary, my brave Mary
You've talked, walked and worked with me!

And I have loved you so.

I have needed you so.
Thank you Mary, my Mary
For walking with me!

O Laama O Laama

Beneath the African sky
We watched the rising sun
From the wide savannah
And celebrated
Our love's journey.
It was there we heard
O Laama! O Laama!
Sweet West African word.
O Laama! O Laama!
Words so meaningful
'It's beautiful! It's beautiful!'
Beneath the rising sun
Our hearts sang as one
O Laama! O Laama!

Beneath the African sky
We watched the golden moon
From the wide savannah
And celebrated
Our love's oneness.
It was there we sang
O Laama! O Laama!
Sweet West African song
O Laama! O Laama!
Praise so enjoyable
'It's beautiful! It's beautiful!'
Beneath the golden moon
Our hearts sang as one
O Laama! O Laama!

Beneath the African sky

We watched the starry night
From the wide savannah
And celebrated
Our love's Saviour.
It was there we prayed
O Laama! O Laama!
Sweet West African praise
O Laama! O Laama!
Grace so powerful
He's beautiful! He's beautiful!
Beneath the starry night
Our hearts sang as one
O Laama! O Laama!

Rainbow in the Mist

There was a rainbow in the mist
As the sunshine touched the spray
Of the falls on the Zambezi river
There we stood,
Hand in hand,
Watching
The rainbow in the mist,
And I knew,
Once again I knew
I loved you
As I've never loved before

There was a rainbow in the mist
As the sunshine touched the spray
Of the falls on the Zambezi river
There we stood
Heart to heart
Hearing
The thunder of the falls
And I knew,
Once again I knew,
I loved you
As I've never loved before.

There was a rainbow in the mist
As the sunshine touched the spray
Of the falls on the Zambezi river
There we stayed,
Arm in arm
Knowing
The wonder of the mist

And I knew,
Once again I knew,
I loved you
As I've never loved before.

The rainbow in the mist
At Victoria Falls
Was a promise
Of love transparent
And true.
The rainbow in the mist
At Victoria Falls
Was the glory
Of love transparent
And true.

Thank You, Thank You

The girl of my dreams
Is there beside me
When I awake
In the mornings
My heart with wonder
Makes me want to say,
With sincerity
And humility
Thank you,
Thank you
Thank you Lord
For this woman
I call my wife.

Along the way
Throughout the day
My mind will say
Thank you
Thank you
Thank you Lord
For this woman,
Who is my wife.

The girl of my dreams
Walked the way with me
Across the years
So faithfully
When I look at her
I simply want to say,
With a heart on fire
With holy desire,

Thank you,
Thank you,
Thank you Lord
For this woman
Who shares my wife.

The girl of my dreams
Will be there for me
When I return
In the evenings.
My heart with delight
Will whisper in the night,
With tenderness
And sweet caress,
Thank you,
Thank you,
Thank you Lord,
For this woman
I call my wife.

You Were There

You were there
With me
In my valley of tears
When my heart
Was breaking,
My way full of fears
You were there
With me,
And I loved you so.

You were there
When I needed
Someone to care,
Someone to share
In the burden of my heart
You were there.

You were there
With me
As I climbed my mountain
When my heart
Was straining
My way filled with pain,
You were there
With me,
And I loved you so.

You were there
When I needed
Someone's strength,
Someone's wisdom
For the burden of my heart
You were there.

You were there
With me
By the springs of life
When my heart
Was saying
My way is free from strife
You were there
With me,
And I loved you so.

You were there
When I needed
Someone's laughter
Someone's warmth
For the hunger of my heart
You were there.

The Gambler

Life is a gamble, that's what people say
And love is just like it in so many ways
Many gamble with love and life
Losing both in sorrow and strife!

Now here I stand
Ready to play the game
Now here I am
Willing and ready
For the chance
To bet my life
On love.

Before I met you
I was so secure,
Contented,
Self assured.
Now everything is changed,
I'm no longer the same,
I'm a gambler
Ready to bet my life
On you,
Only you!

Now here I stand
Ready to give my love
Now here I go
Willing and ready
For the chance
To bet my life
On you.

I'm a gambler
In the game of love.
I've given my all;
I've taken the chance;
I've bet my future,
My life,
My love,
On you,
Only you...
    And this I know
I've gambled
And won!

You, Me and the Letter 'V'

I know my ABC
Through to XYZ
But it's the letter 'V'
Which best reveals you
To me
In variegated ways!

You're my valentine
Every day of the year
Without question
The only one
Who alone could vanquish
My insane vanity!

You're as soft velvet
To this body of mine
Vibrant in venery
Vivacious visually
My heart's vitality
And virtue's integrity!

Mary's my vineyard
My eternal valentine
More delightful than wine
My soul's intoxication,
My constant fascination
That's you, me and the letter 'V'

The Photograph

Hello my precious wife
How are you today?
Guess what?
I'm talking to your photograph
'cause I'm missing you.
The snapshot is in a lovely setting
But doesn't capture the beauty
Of the person shown.
No painting or photograph
Captures the radiance of love
The vivaciousness of a smile
Let alone the skin's fragrance
Or the lips enchantment

That reflected image
Frozen in time
Creates
Sensations deep within
'cause I'm missing you.
The picture is professionally done
But cannot reveal your spirit
The sweetness of a look
The sound of your voice
Nor the power of a wink
As I gaze on the photograph
I'm acutely aware
How precious you are.

That silent photograph
Hold memories
Unnumbered

Stirs gratitude to God
Tho' I'm missing you
The camera has captured you
Only externally
Still, it causes me to drink
Again of your attractiveness,
To recall togetherness
With God's faithfulness,
But I must confess,
I'm still missing you!

I Forgot to Remember

I remember
What I forgot!
What did I forget
To remember?

My wife,
She asked me
To remember her birthday
But I forgot
Until today.

But

Her birthday
Was yesterday
And I remembered
Today.
What can I say?

Will I
remember
To apologise?
When I see her tomorrow
Or just cry?

Oh dear

How silly of me
Her birthday
I remember
Is in September
This is November!

Did she

Remember
Her birthday
Or like me
Fail to recall
The date she was born?

Doubtful.

How then
Can I remember
Her birthday
From now
        To September.

Background Music

Softly,
Caressing my ears,
Enhancing the silence
Surrounding my being,
The music plays.

You are
Background music,
Enriching my aloneness,
Encompassing my life
Where—ever I may be.

Tuned
To your wave length
My heart hears
No other's music,
No siren's song.

Years
Creep slowly by,
The music continues
Sensuous, sweet,
Love's melody.

Because
You're constantly
In my foreground
You'll ever remain
My background music.

Funny Isn't It

Funny isn't it
How my heart beats
Faster
When you're near!

Scary isn't it
How
The heart cries
Sadly
When you're away!

Silly isn't it
How
The heart hungers
Always
For your presence!

Lovely isn't it
How
My heart desires
Nothing
Outside of you!

Heavenly isn't it
How
Our hearts beat
Together
Because of love!

Green Eyed Fire

The gleam within green eyes
Sparkle with warmth
Aflame with compassion
Aglow from devotion
Their glance ...
    Enveloped me
    Possessed me
    Consumed me.

The blaze within green eyes
Burns with delight
Aflame with emotion
Aglow from passion
Their look ...
    Penetrates my heart
    Stimulates my dreams
    Exhilarates my mind

The flames within green eyes
Fuelled with love
Aflame with faithfulness
Aglow from tenderness
Their sight ...
    Un–dampened by tears
    Undaunted by fears
    Unconcerned by sneers.

The fire within green eyes
Set my life alight
Torched my darkness
Melted my coldness
Burned my aloofness
... I love her green eyed fire.

You're Always In My Heart

You're always in my heart,
When near
Or far away.
You're always in my dreams
You're my
Only theme.
You're always in my heart
Always
In my dreams.

You, only you are ...
Love's treasure,
My pleasure
Beyond measure
In my heart,
In my dreams.

You're always on my mind
In sun
Or moonshine.
You're always in my prayers
Knowing our
Saviour cares.
You're always on my mind,
Always
In my prayers.

You, only you are ...
Love inspiring

My desiring
Joy supplying
In my mind
In my prayers.

You're always in my heart,
In my dreams.
You're always on my mind
In my prayers
Because,
I love you so!

Looking Back on Love

Looking back on love,
Across the landscape of life,
Roads travelled,
Experiences felt,
Burdens shared,
Pleasures
Beyond measure
So many memories
Begging for attention
From the day
Love began,
A day
On which
The sun has never set.

Looking back on love
From the hilltop of age
Is the privilege
Of senior years
Mountains climbed
Valleys crossed
Dreams fulfilled,
Hopes delayed,
Love known,
Shown,
Always
From the day
Love's sun rose on us.

Love Thoughts

Unannounced
They stride into the mind
Unconcerned
About other occupants.
Undaunted,
They steal the centre-stage.
Unmolested
Across the landscape they roam.

Unquenchable
Their flames of passion.
Undisguised,
The images they create.
Unforgettable
The memories birthed,
Undeniable
The impact upon the soul.

Unfailing
The awe generated.
Undeniable,
The joy of their presence.
Unconquerable
The inspiration aroused,
Undying
The power of Love Thoughts.

One Day at a Time

You took my hand and smiled
Your eyes sparkled,
Light reflecting
A rainbow from a tear
Nestling on the lash
As you said
You loved me
And would be mine
Forever.
That is such a long, long time
But I will enjoy it
One day at a time
Forever.

I took you in my arms
My eyes flashed
Light revealing
A cascade of tears
Across my cheeks
As I said
I loved you
And would be yours
Forever.
That is such a long, long time
But I'll give it to you
One day at a time
Forever.

By God's grace
We will love
Each other
One day at a time,
Forever!

The Seat in the Park

The seat in the park
Was occupied,
An older couple
Close together.
He in casual gear
Peaked hat, scarf.
She, coat and skirt
With matching shawl
He wore a smile,
She, a faraway look
Hand in hand,
Wordless,
Contented,
There they sat.

The seat in the park,
A lovers' patch
For reverie
The silence
Onlookers felt
Contained memories
Conveyed
By closeness
No words needed.
His smile,
Her look
Reflected love
Perfumed
By the years.

The seat in the park

Holy ground
For these two
Young in heart
Strong in trust
Enjoying each others
Quietness
An eloquent
Testimony
Of journeys
Together
Hand in hand
Doing
God's pleasure.

It Hasn't Been Easy

It hasn't been easy over the years,
I'm sure you'll agree,
It hasn't been easy seeing those tears
We've shed together
But,
We've come through stronger
Wiser and bolder.
How did we do it people want to know?
How did we face life with its many blows?

The secret,
It's very simple really.
What gave us the strength to carry on?
What helped us see a new tomorrow?
What gave us the hope that caused our smile?
What made all the tough times seem worthwhile?
Love!

It hasn't been easy on you or me,
I'm sure you'll agree,
It hasn't been easy handling the pace
Stressing you and me
But,
We've come through with God's grace
Grateful and joyful.
How did we do it people want to know?
How did we handle life when we were low?

The secret,
Is really quiet beautiful
What's the bond holding us together?
What's the joy that will last forever?

What's the gift we've given each other?
What's the peace that nothing can smother?
Love!

We Love Because ...

1 John 4:19

We love because
 God first loved us.
His love claimed our lives
Through the Christ of Calvary
Moulding our lives patiently
To obey Him faithfully!

We love because
 God first loved us.
He blended our lives together
To enjoy love's majesty
Within every–day's history
Sharing unbroken intimacy!

We love because
 God first loved us.
He prepared us by His word
A common purpose to share
To know and serve the Lord
Until we meet Him in the air!

How Can it Be

How can it be
We would stay in love
To celebrate
Fifty years of marriage?
That's no mystery
Simply love's majesty

How can it be?
You ask that of me
It is no secret
It plain for all to see
Love breeds commitment
Love feeds adjustment

How can it be?
We've blessed each other
By mutual trust
Closer now than ever
With passion's dedication
And pleasure's adoration

For these fifty years
A prayer of gratitude
From my heart and lips
For God's precious gift
Of my wife and friend
That's
How it can be!

To love, honour and obey
Each other paves the way
Through kindly gestures

And deliberate measures
Esteeming each other
That's
How it can be!

Years have their history
Passion ebbs, love glows
Age slows, wonder grows
We both belong to Christ
Who gave each the other
That's
How it can be!

Also available from Ray Hawkins

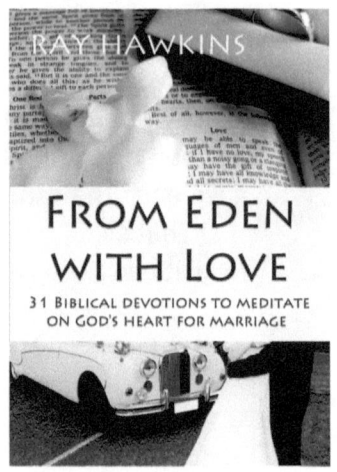

From Eden with Love
31 Biblical devotionals to meditate on God's heart for marriage.
ISBN: 978-1-921633-41-6
Be taken on a tour of the Majesty of Marriage through 31 days of 'From Eden with Love.' Discover the Heavenly mystery underpinning the meaning of the Christian Marriage.

www.evenbeforepublishing.com

www.ingramcontent.com/pod-product-compliance
Lightning Source LLC
Chambersburg PA
CBHW021119080526
44587CB00010B/569